Struggled to Sold

A Real Estate Broker's Journey and Guide On How to Launch a Real Estate Brokerage & Sell in 5 Years

Madeline A Rousseau

Dedication

This book is dedicated to my boys: Daniel and Stephen!! The Loves of my Life!

They had no idea then that they were my motivation every single day and still are today. My reason for getting out of bed every morning and for me wanting to better myself every day.

I had mouths to feed then and bills to pay. I wanted them to have a childhood and life that they deserved. I didn't want them to see my struggle. But, I know they did. They were my biggest supporters and biggest fans!! And, still are to this day! I wanted to make them proud and lead by example always staying in the light. They may have seen my struggle but they also witnessed their mother Rise, Shine and Thrive!

This is my most favorite song that I have dedicated to my sons over the years. "My Wish" by Rascal Flats.

My wish, for you, is that this life becomes all that you want it to. your DREAMS stay BIG, and your worries stay small, you never need to carry more than you can hold, and while you are out there getting where you are going to.... I HOPE You know somebody LOVES YOU

This photo is the first photo taken after my divorce in 2002 with just Mom and Boys. We jumped quickly into one of those little photo booths that you pay $5.00 for in the middle of a mall and this is what would be the start of "Mom and Boys Always."

They are grown men now and will always be the lights of my life!

FOURTH PLATOON
DG SANDAL
GS TORRES
ESSON
Queens via
Bway Local
To Ditmars Bl
Astoria
all times

My little Family
4 Generations!!

Acknowledgment

I want to recognize and express my utmost gratefulness to the special and supportive people throughout my journey. I would like to thank my mentors and influencers who inspired me to always take it to the next level bettering myself and to those who helped me in the creation of this book. There have been many who provided inspiration and guidance, some that won't be mentioned. Every single person that I've met and have spent time with cannot get mentioned because the list would be miles long! But, they know who they are and are probably reading this right now because of their support always.

My Mother: She's been in my life the longest and the one that I call every day. She's seen it all. My rise and fall and my highs and lows. She always inspires me to do my best. What I have I get from her. She is the strongest woman I know and always there unconditionally- I always say "I get it from my Momma." I've always been in awe of her strength and courage. She gave birth to me very young leaving high school. She had all the qualities I possess today and rose to the top. Proud of my Mom for her selflessness, resilience and determination. Life didn't come with a manual when I was born but it did come with a Mother and I got the best! Thankful to my mom for always listening and for all of the encouragement throughout my life. Without her this book wouldn't exist.

My Father: Has passed away but he instilled a work ethic in me like no other and gave me the entrepreneurial spirit that got me here. He was the only one that would send me flowers every Valentine's Day with a note "Will you be my Valentine?" He encouraged me to be a business owner from the very beginning. He is missed.

Daniel and Stephen: My children mean more to me than anyone! This book I dedicated to them because of their unwavering love and support. Always encouraging their Mother to live her best life! God blessed me with two of the best sons a Mother could ever ask for and I'm thankful for them, they own my heart!

Thankful to my sister and brother and to all of my Family and Friends who offered emotional support and encouragement over the years. To those I leaned on for mentorship like my friend Greg Kelly, Broker/Owner of Sellstate Superior in The Villages, Florida and my friend Bill Houle who now owns his own real estate brokerage called BHIVE Realty in Ocala, Florida. If I listed all of my family, friends and why I'd be writing another book!

I'd like to acknowledge and thank Steve Jahn. Steve was the catalyst- the wonderfully kind man who said "Come meet me in Islamorada, you may not want to leave." I believe God places special people in our lives at certain times for very specific reasons. I was searching for the island life and to live in paradise. Because of Steve, I found it. For the last 2 years he's been my best friend, one of my biggest supporters and encouragers. The first to encourage me to write this book! I value him, our special friendship and the fun adventures we've had living here in Islamorada!

I am very thankful to my publisher here and the team provided that included editors, proofreaders who polished the manuscript, designers and my project manager Mark who helped bring this book to life! I am now a published author thanks to all of them!! I am grateful for the collaborative efforts behind the book and want to acknowledge and show them appreciation because they played a pivotal role in this book's development!

Contents

Page Blank Intentionally

Endorsements

I am writing to offer my highest recommendation and deepest admiration for Madeline Rousseau, the former owner and broker of Keys to the Bay Real Estate. Her tenure as the owner and broker of Keys to the Bay Real Estate was marked by remarkable achievements and an unwavering commitment to excellence, setting an exceptional standard in the real estate industry.

Madeline's leadership and vision transformed Keys to the Bay Real Estate into a powerhouse of success. She organized and executed numerous highly successful events, fostering a sense of community and collaboration among her agents. These events not only showcased her innovative approach to real estate but also provided invaluable learning and networking opportunities for everyone involved.

Her hands-on approach and dedication to her team were truly inspirational. Madeline was always there to guide, mentor, and support her agents, helping many of them achieve their own professional milestones, including obtaining their broker's licenses. Her ability to identify and nurture talent was unparalleled, and she played a pivotal role in shaping the careers of countless realtors.

Madeline has been a standout broker and an inspiration to so many in the real estate business. Her passion, dedication, and innovative mindset have left an indelible mark on all who had the privilege of working with her. Her new book is sure to be a testament to her remarkable journey and the countless lives she has positively impacted.

I am honored to have witnessed Madeline's extraordinary contributions to our industry and look forward to seeing her continue to inspire and lead through her writing and future endeavors.

Sincerely,

Joel Erlichson

Author, Realtor, and Mortgage Loan Originator

RE/MAX

I'm thrilled to endorse Madeline Rousseau's book, which is a testament to her remarkable journey of personal growth and professional success. Her story of building a thriving brokerage from scratch and eventually selling it is a true inspiration, and a reminder that hard work, determination, and resilience can lead to achieving even the most ambitious goals.

Veronica Henderson

Keys to The Bay Real Estate

vron801@hotmail.com

mailto:vron801@hotmail.com

210-473-3566

I had the pleasure of working under Madeline as a new agent and can confidently say that she is a role model in the real estate industry. She is a combination of deep knowledge, unwavering confidence, and action-taking.

Madeline is not only an amazing broker, she is an inspiring mentor and leader. Her guidance has been invaluable in shaping my career, mentoring me from my first transaction and now a high-producing agent in my market.

Andrew Seickel,

Realtor

I feel fortunate to have Madeline Rousseau as a friend and mentor, especially during the time as my real estate broker.

I vividly remember our first meeting over lunch a few years ago, where she shared her vision of starting a network marketing group that included me. At the time, I was focused on my online business and exploring new opportunities. Little did I know then how profoundly she would impact my life.

Madeline's genuine presence and heartfelt conversations were instrumental in expanding our group, and I quickly formed many meaningful connections. Her encouragement pushed me out of my comfort zone and greatly boosted my confidence. Inspired by her, I decided to pursue my real estate license. Passing the state exam on my first attempt was a pivotal moment that I eagerly shared with her. It marked the beginning of a new chapter for both of us: she was embarking on a new life in Islamorada, while I was launching my career as a licensed realtor.

Despite the distance, Madeline often visited Tampa, where we established a successful business relationship, collaborating on various real estate deals. I am grateful for her mentoring and feel privileged to have learned from the best.

When she informed me of her decision to sell her brokerage, I was delighted to see her pursue her dreams of living in paradise and embarking on a new journey of sharing her real estate expertise to educate and mentor others.

Denise Rojas,

Realtor

Madeline always amazes me. I have watched her build two highly successful real estate brokerages. Her absolute attention to detail and willingness to lead her teams by example has been nothing short of inspiring. I now have my own brokerage and I can say that Madeline has shown me a road map to my success and inspired me to never give up on my dreams.

William Houle

Broker/Owner

BHIVE Realty

Preface

With this book, I intend to inspire others with my story. To encourage others to not be afraid and to have the courage to take their life and career to the next level especially those in Real Estate. I want to share and show how I was able to overcome life's obstacles because going through life's challenges often resemble the unpredictable journey in real estate. It's essential to view failures as stepping stones to success. I was there and now I'm here showing how I was able to rebuild my life and build a real estate company to sell and will provide insight, advice and steps along with a helpful guide for those interested in deeper insights on how to grow and succeed by upping their game.

My success was built from the ground up. It seems like a lot but it's entirely possible with the right mindset. Whether you're just starting out or looking for the next step up - the key is to build a solid foundation.

I'm giving practical advice here from my heart and from my own experiences of truly starting over- building myself and my career from the ground up. I hope this encourages you to start transforming your career today. This isn't just another business book or guide, it's a blueprint for success in a very changing, shifting, dynamic industry where we help others through our work.

Introduction

I was there, and now I'm here—living my dream in Paradise. My journey has led me to a place where I can help others through my work, every single day. Inspiring others has always been my aspiration, and now it's my reality.

With 15 years of Real Estate experience and ownership of 4 Companies over the years, my philosophy is simple: To help others through my work by providing exceptional service and personalized attention to clients and Realtors alike. I believe that every client and every Realtor is unique and deserves a customized approach to their real estate needs and careers.

My life journey landed me in a tropical paradise, a transformation that has been profoundly inspiring. I love Islamorada and The Florida Keys. Surrounded by peace and natural beauty, I am inspired to create something truly special here—something that will help and inspire others to live their best lives and elevate their careers to the next level.

I can barely believe it myself, but after years of hard work and determination, I am finally living my dream! I am so grateful to be able to wake up every morning in this beautiful place I call home and do what I love. My passion is helping others, and I am fortunate to be able to do so through my work.

"Helping Others Through My Work" is not just a tagline—it's a core value that defines who I am. Inspiring others to chase their dreams has always been a passion of mine, and I am deeply grateful for the opportunity to make a difference in the lives of those around me.

Chapter One

We all know that the struggle is real! As time marches on the future has been on my mind—how to best navigate it, fulfill my purpose and give back in meaningful ways. The Real Estate game has shifted, and I'd like to share my story, focusing on creating a valuable resource that will guide and motivate individuals to chase their dreams and find success.

I believe the best place to start for this would be to start literally from the beginning.

My name is Madeline Ann RUSSO – ROUSSEAU. Yes! Different last name pronounced the same. I am currently the sole owner and broker of Madeline Rousseau Real Estate, located in the upper Florida Keys at MM 88- Islamorada. I was born in Queens, Long Island, NY on a Sunday at 5:01 PM, March 6, 1966 under a full moon. This is probably why I am such a Moon lover. My mother 18 and still in High School, and my father was 20. Unmarried until I was 3, my maternal grandparents cared for me while my Mom worked. To this day, my Grandpa Frank is the most special person in my life. I believe he is up in the heavens, always watching over me and nudging me in the right direction.

My parents married in 1969, and my sister was born. Our family then moved to Ft. Lauderdale, Florida, where my brother was later born. We lived in the same home for 16 years, and I completed all of my school years there, graduating from St. Thomas Aquinas High School. This is where I say I grew up! Even after all these years, I still remember my home address: 1251 NW 56th Ave. and my phone number too: 305-587-8107.

Thanks to my Dad, I grew up in a shop and was quite tom boyish, loving riding dirt bikes, 4-wheelers, go-karts and building forts. I was taught to change oil, batteries, tires and was driving by the age of 11. I learned how to drive on a stick shift by my dad and shortly thereafter was driving around in a tow truck picking up cars. I was also very athletic. I played Tennis, thanks to my mom as she loved playing tennis. I played Volleyball and Softball in school. I loved softball. My Aunt Annabelle took me under her wing and taught me how to play. I was a very good player with a strong throw so I played 3rd base and catcher. God blessed me with two boys for a reason—I was meant to be a boy mom!

Shortly after I graduated high school at the age of 19, my mom and dad moved our little family away from the rest of the family—out of what we thought was a city to an unfamiliar country place that no one heard of in North Central Florida, called Ocala. We didn't even know how to pronounce the name of the city then. In 1985, it was nothing but cows, dirt and horse farms. Now, many years later, Ocala, in Marion County is very well-known and considered the Horse Capital of the World.

I was young, still working with my family in the used car business, trying to figure out where I belonged and what I was meant to do. In 1987, I met my ex-husband, and we married in December of 1990. When we met, he was an E-5 MP in the Army's Green to Gold program, attending college to obtain a BA in Criminal Justice and become a Commissioned Officer. That goal was accomplished as he graduated and was Commissioned as a 2nd Lieutenant. Two weeks later, we had a full-on Catholic military wedding, swords and all, with a big spank on the bottom welcoming me to the Army. At that moment I became an officer's wife, and my life began to change. Around the same time, "Desert Storm" kicked off, and there was a lot of uncertainty about what would happen and where we would go. Deployed or not deployed?

The military too had no idea and we were placed on hold but could not go anywhere too far. Even though we were considered active duty, we weren't, which lasted for six months. No pay, no assignment, no insurance. We moved to Maitland, Florida, outside of Orlando, and because we were on hold, a job waiting tables at the Olive Garden sustained us. Two months later, we received the news that we were expecting our first baby—without insurance. Almost six months later, the Army figured it out: no deployment and our first assignment would be at Schofield Barracks in Honolulu, Hawaii, but first, two short schools must be attended before getting there.

So, my parents paid for my first pregnancy office visit, nervous that we had no insurance. All was good to go as we moved what little we had to Weaver, Alabama, living in a basement rental for four months so that he could attend an MP Officer Basic course at Ft. McClellan, which is now closed. He was very excited to show me our new place for four months, and all I could do was cry. I had just moved out of a 5,000-square-foot house with 5 bedrooms on 5 acres, and now I was living in a basement!

Our vehicle was shipped, so thankfully, with a family in the car business, my parents let us borrow a vehicle from the car lot that they happily towed to Alabama, assuring us it had a working AC. AC is important in Florida, but now we are into fall, and another short two-month course was thrown in there before heading to Hawaii, so we started our drive with everything we owned to Ft. Knox, KY. I was now very pregnant, and it snows in Kentucky. Even though our borrowed vehicle had great AC, no one thought about checking the heat. I laugh because I froze driving that Florida vehicle—thanks, Mom and Dad!!

We were in Kentucky for about two months, living outside of Ft. Knox as the days marched on and grew cooler. We had one borrowed vehicle, so a couple days a week, there was a carpool so that I could have the vehicle for use. When I didn't have the vehicle, as I was getting more pregnant, I would walk. There was this ceramic shop full of German women who loved me and took me in, feeding me all of the time. Everyone in my family and all of my friends received ceramics that year, made and painted by me for Christmas—laughing again as I remember that time in my life. Our time in Kentucky was coming to an end, and I was about 6 weeks from delivering our first child. We had our flights booked, parents picking up the borrowed vehicle, and personal belongings scheduled for shipment to Hawaii.

My last doctor's visit on the mainland in KY revealed that airlines don't accept travelers over 6 months pregnant! I was not staying in KY giving birth alone! I walked out of the doctor's office that day with a note saying I was less than six months pregnant, advised to wear tight pantyhose, leave shoes on, and pray I don't go into labor over the water—and if I did, pray for a doctor on the flight with us, which was a total of nine hours.

We landed safely in Honolulu, Hawaii, transitioning from very cold weather to very hot weather. As I sat on the plane, preparing to exit, my feet began to swell, so there was no removing my shoes for sure. We were excited to meet our hosts, who picked us up at the airport. They set up accommodations for us until we could get housing on Schofield Barracks, and they happily drove us there with a stop for lunch on the North Shore. Hawaii is hot. Most everything in Hawaii was open-air, including restaurants, malls, etc. Our hotel had no AC. I didn't think I would survive as I started swelling up like a balloon, but thankfully, our sponsors were kind enough to place us in another hotel with AC.

There was no on-post housing with a year-long wait. So, the house hunting began! Hawaii was and is very expensive. We were lucky to find off post housing that we could afford in Makakilo Cliffs at $1,100.00 a month then. As soon as we arrived at our new apartment, and tried to settle in, a two-week deployment happened, leaving me alone to manage. I sold off all of my ex-husbands stuff because our apartment was so small nothing would fit when it got delivered. I laugh because he was not happy about that. When you leave a very pregnant woman at home alone that's what happens. Our apartment was so small! You walked in the front door of the apartment and out the back door. But, the view was amazing.

Chapter Two

On December 24, Christmas Eve, 1991, our first son, Daniel Thomas Jr., was born in Honolulu, Hawaii, at Tripler Medical Center- the Pink Hospital. It was the best Christmas gift ever! The gift of life that Daniel brought into my world was truly the best present any parent could ask for.

I loved living in Hawaii for almost 3 years! In the end, I flew out again, very pregnant with the same advice as before, as we headed back to Weaver, AL, for yet another school. Shortly thereafter, our second son, Stephen Leo, was born on October 11, 1994, in Jacksonville Hospital, Alabama. Another beautiful gift from God! He was a tiny little nugget when we packed up yet again and moved to Killeen, TX. We lived there for a year. Then Carmel, Indiana, for a year, Newburgh, Indiana, for 3 years, and then Maine.

We lived in Maine for a total of 3 years. After 1 year in Maine, I became divorced. Their dad had resigned his commission from the Army but was still a Government employee. With that being said he was gone a lot. At this point I decided to stay in Maine which lasted 2 years as to not pull the boys away from their dad so that when he was "home" they could see him. Life was not easy living in Maine by myself with 2 boys. It was very expensive and very cold for months and months. I found myself buying groceries on my credit card in the winter just so I could by oil for the gas tank to provide heat. It snowed in Maine and when it snowed it snowed! We were locked down. The ice storms were crazy and driving on black ice almost killed me twice! After 3 years, their dad was finally getting transferred out of Maine to a different location. There was no reason for me to follow him around anymore and I wanted the boys to have a home to grow roots and I knew it could not be Maine. Maine was beautiful in the summer and fall, July-Oct. Their dad and I both decided it was best for me to move back "home" to Ocala, Florida to be by my family and to have a nice home base for the boys to grow up and to rebuild my life.

I have lived in many places in the United States. I was away from Florida, the place I called home, for 14 years. I left Ocala, Florida, in 1990, saying I would never go back. In 2004, I moved back to Ocala from Maine, which I called the Frozen North. This time, divorced, with 2 boys - 7 and 10 years old in tow. I supported my boys' father all those years. Being an Officer's wife and a stay-at-home mother to our boys, sacrificing an education and work experience, but I wouldn't trade those years for anything! There is a lot in between all of that, but that will have to be another book sometime down the road. I share these little bits of my life with you to show you how I was there. Young. Married. Divorced. 2 kids and their father away most of the time. No education. No job, with 10 years of no work history.

At the age of 38, back in Ocala, it was time to figure it all out and rebuild my life. Easy, right? I promised the boys I would not move them again so that they could grow roots! Our welcome to Florida in July was heat, humidity, and five back-to-back hurricanes! My boys wanted to move back to Maine, especially after they had to put their heads between their knees at school with the storm-tornado warnings. I cried and cried, sweating profusely as I had been in Maine for 3 years, not used to the heat and humidity. My dad would say go back to Maine then! But I promised the boys I wouldn't move them, and I didn't. I had the help of my family, which I and the boys desperately needed at the time.

A lot of people see me and my success today at this stage of my life, 20 years later, and where I am now, but have no idea what it took to get here, with all the trials and tribulations along the way.

They don't know about the countless nights I spent crying myself to sleep, the endless days of uncertainty, or the moments of pure exhaustion. But they also don't know about the moments of pure joy, the triumphs, and the sense of accomplishment that I feel today.

The comeback is always more powerful than the setback. A lot of steps forward then backward, but the key is always persistently moving forward no matter what. In my eyes, the key to success is persisting through these challenges and continuously moving forward, no matter how difficult it may seem.

At 38, I decided to go back to school and finish my BA. Originally, way back when, I started in Accounting. Things have changed since then, and I wanted to help others and give back, so I applied to the Social Work program and was accepted at UCF. UCF had a satellite campus in Ocala, but no Social Work classes were offered there, and I had no desire to travel to Orlando for classes. I then switched it up, and after 6 years of working, raising boys, and going to classes part-time, I finally graduated with my BA in Psychology with a minor in Social Work. I had a full-time accounting job as I got through school. I had to set a good example as I couldn't expect my sons to bring home good grades and Mom not. They saw me study, write papers, take tests! They would encourage me, wish me luck, and root for me as I would do for them. There were plenty of times, exhausted, I asked myself why I was torturing myself wanting to throw in the towel. But I didn't. I graduated at the age of 43 with honors. Proud moment. Education goal achieved.

My sons were getting older, teenagers, driving, and soon to leave the nest at some point, sooner now than later. I thought I wanted to work in psychology as a Psychologist, but to achieve that goal, I would have to continue my schooling for at least 2-3 more years to obtain a master's degree. I wasn't making the money in my accounting job that I needed to make and literally hated it! Someone mentioned to me once that I would make a great real estate agent. It was never on my list of things to do or to pursue.

In 2009, as I was working in accounting full time, spending time with family, and barely making my bills, someone I met was studying to take the real estate exam. I helped him study for hours and hours, going through the whole course with him just to be helpful. Creating study cards and going over and over them. Lo and behold, there was a newly licensed real estate agent as he passed the state exam first try! At that moment I realized I knew as much as he did and decided to do it myself- what the heck, right? I could work full-time and do the real estate part-time on the side and make some extra money. How hard can it be? Everyone asked me then why I was getting into real estate when everyone was getting out with the market crash. I signed up for the real estate course, giving myself a goal of 2 months to complete. It ended up taking 6 months thanks to a little medical emergency that ended in my gall bladder being removed. But I passed the course exam and was ready.

After making an application to the State of Florida for a Real Estate license and finishing up my background check and fingerprinting, I scheduled myself to take the State exam. I failed the state test by 2 questions. I went right back in and took it again, failing it again by 1 question. How can he pass this test and not me? I was getting frustrated. I just graduated with a degree in Psychology and worked in accounting. Real estate was very different. Something I knew absolutely nothing about except for what I read in my books. I literally had to know more than you would expect to pass this test! Appraising, surveying, plumbing, electrical, contractor stuff, mortgages, and the math, I hate math! And the list goes on. I did not let this test get to me, and on the third try, I passed!

So then it began!! Working my accounting job full-time and real estate part-time nights, weekends and on my lunch breaks. The real estate market was not what it is today!!

The market turned difficult, and buyers and homeowners needed help most. I was thrown into the fire and learned real estate the hard way, specializing in short sales and foreclosures. I started my career hanging my license with an independently owned franchise, Keller Williams, in Ocala.

My first transaction was buying my own home! I bought a brand new spec home that had been sitting for a couple years, and because I had a real estate license, they paid me a 3% commission. I believe it was $4,500.00. I noted that if I never did anything else with my license it had already paid off because that was extra money I did not count on! I was able to put on gutters, paint the inside, put up fans that were not included with that extra money, and buy some furnishings as every penny I saved went towards the house purchase.

Homeowners were angry, upside down in their homes, losing jobs and not being able to make the payments, and losing whatever equity they may have had. It was not a good time for homeowners; thus, short sales and foreclosures were plentiful. Buyers could purchase homes at very low prices, which was beneficial for them and new home buyers, but if you wanted a home that was under a short sale, it was literally not a "short sale" and would take a very long time to get through the process, sometimes up to a year.

I became the short sale queen. I was selling homes for $17,000, $25,000, $50,000…. Investors were having a field day buying up, putting lipstick on a pig, sort of speaking, and reselling for a profit until the banks figured out how they could do it themselves. My commission checks were $300.00, $600.00, $1,000.00. I prayed for a sale over $100,000, which didn't happen often, so that I could make a decent commission. For me, it didn't matter. It was all the extra money that I could spend on my boys for vacation or new furniture. I became, in what the industry calls 'A Top Producer.'

I was smart enough to bank money, too, saving up so that I could quit my accounting job at some point that I so disliked. I was punching a clock, stuck in an office with no windows, punching numbers all day! With real estate I was outdoors, riding around, meeting different people. That's what I enjoyed most. I continued to do real estate. The part-time work soon became full-time and I got busier. Now, I'm working 2 full-time jobs and 2 kids at home. I realized I was wearing myself out. After 2 years and some courage, I quit my full-time accounting job to pursue real estate full-time. It was scary! No constant paycheck coming in every Friday, no medical benefits, and no retirement.

I was now considered an independent contractor. However, I knew in my heart that if I put 100% of my time into my real estate business, I would do well. I told myself, what's the worst that can happen? I fall flat on my face and would find another accounting job. That was definitely my motivation, knowing I did not want to work ever again in an office with no windows, punching numbers all day!! My boys at home were also my biggest motivation! They inspired me more than they will ever know. They would help me, riding along with me to meet clients and show homes. Put out listing signs, take photos, etc., and it was fun with them! I also jumped ship and left Keller Williams when I went full time to an independently owned ReMax franchise in 2012.

The market started to come back up slowly, very slowly. Nonetheless, the market was getting better, and for two years, I hustled and hustled and hustled, putting all of my energies into real estate and helping others through my work. Every day, there were different challenges with deals that closed and deals that didn't close. I learned quickly how to solve problems! A realtor is also known as a Problem Solver and Jack of all trades! Nothing like getting ready for closing and, on the final walk-through in heels and a dress, bending under a kitchen sink to fix a plumbing issue. And the list goes on.

Chapter Three

For two years, non-stop, I worked and became what we call in the industry a "Top Producer." Back then, in Ocala, it was a downed market, and I had 45 sales/transactions under my belt in a year. That's a lot of work! My total gross sales volume was about 4 million. Today, that 45 transaction year would gross easily 15 million or more. If I was doing the volume today that I was doing then at our current sales prices, I wouldn't have to work another day from here on out.

As 2013 was coming to an end, after 4 years or so of making a name for myself, hustling, and becoming a top producer, I realized I was losing a lot of money paying all of the individually owned Broker fees/splits and transaction fees that were then getting implemented and franchise fees. I was losing close to 40-50% of my commissions. At this point, I had spoken to my broker about getting on a better split to keep more of my commissions in my own pocket as my expenses were going up as well. Some brokerages were becoming more competitive and offering better compensation plans. I was denied by the broker, generally stating that if we do it for you, we have to do it for everyone. That did not set well with me. No reward for bettering yourself. There was no reward for the experience I now had. I felt like I paid my dues and did my time, sort of speak. I wasn't a brand new agent any longer and now a Top

Producer that was being heavily recruited. I had about 30 active listings under my name at that time.

I thought to myself then about bettering myself and taking this real estate gig to the next level. I reflected on my strengths and weaknesses and brainstorming ways to enhance my skills and knowledge in the industry. I was determined to push myself beyond my limits and make a name for myself in the competitive world of real estate.

So, after that conversation and without hesitation, I signed up for the Brokers Course, studying yet again, but now that I had worked in Real Estate for 4 years, the course seemed easier as I understood more. I passed the course and passed the State exam on the first try.

During all of this, I had been working with an investor who was buying and selling houses. He heard of me passing and becoming a Broker and offered to partner with me to open a Brokerage. He was very convincing. I thought, why not? My father said, don't do it with a partner. I should have listened to him then. But, I felt like he was someone I could trust at the time. Without even knowing what I was doing, I created an LLC, applied for an EIN and a CQ license, drew up a partnership agreement, created a logo, found office space, and boom!

Very quickly, I was the Owner and Broker of my first Real

Estate company. I was also a working Realtor, basically the one making the Company money. I just added all that extra work on to my plate. The benefit was being able to keep more of my own commissions in my pocket and not have to answer to anyone outside of my partner. And, to say hey, I'm the Owner and Broker of my own company! My credibility just went up tenfold!! The benefit for my partner was having a company he could put his own deals through along with a worker bee to do all of the work! He was that silent partner, sort of speak and I was, as my mom says, the worker bee.

I had then advised all of my clients that I had passed my broker's test and was opening up my own brokerage. All of them were excited and genuinely happy for me. The 30-plus sellers that had their homes/properties listed with me all wanted to make certain that I kept their listings, which, of course, I thought would be easy. The brokerage owns all listings. If you leave a Brokerage, they can keep your listings. I learned very quickly that those sellers were listing with me because of me, not because of the brokerage. Their faith was in me and my expertise/knowledge. They all genuinely knew me, liked me and trusted me.

Thankfully, all of my listings, with the exception of one short sale, were moved over to my new company. Not without being proactive first. The old brokerage didn't want to release the listings. I had all of my clients sign cancellation of listing agreements. Then, all of them had a zero-dollar cancel fee. I always explain to my clients that if, for some reason, they were not happy with me or I could not get their home or property sold in a timely matter, and they wanted to cancel their listing agreement with me, I would not charge them for that. It was my job to sell their property, and that's exactly what I would do.

Once the listings were transferred to my new company, new signage had to be created and a new website and marketing had to be created. There is definitely some up-front money needed to start a Brokerage and carry a lot of listings.

In all honesty, this whole time, I literally winged it to success. Learning by doing. Mistakes were made along the way, but they taught me a lot. My partner and I brought on another Realtor as a partner and now there were three of us. We were moving along nicely, adding Realtors to the company, and it was growing nicely. I learned quickly that 3 business partners all agreeing was not easy. We would have to have monthly meetings and vote.

Our original partner started to disagree a lot and was voted down 2-1. This was causing him to rear up an ugly side and he decided to go sideways on us. He was trying to bully, extort money and threatened us. The end result was dissolving the company and starting a new one with just the 2 of us as partners. The court was involved for 3 years with the original partner. It was a lot of work, but we managed to create another Company and move on with it nicely. This company was given to my partner 2 years later due to me making a brave move to downtown Tampa, and that company today is still in business and owned by that partner in Ocala.

While all this was happening, things in my personal life were changing. My children left the nest to pursue their dreams. I had no idea how hard that life moment would be. The empty nest syndrome is real. They both left the nest at the same time. My oldest son, Daniel, finished 2 years at the Community College in Ocala and was offered an EMT job in Washington, DC. I'll never forget the moment when he said see you soon, Mom and jumped in a U-Haul truck with everything he called his and waved goodbye. I held those tears back till I couldn't see the truck any longer, and then I cried my eyes out!

My youngest son was accepted to USF in Tampa and was moving into his dorm. Again, holding back the tears until I left him there without him coming back for a while. I promised them when we moved in 2004 that I would not move them again, all the while knowing when they left, I would probably leave too. But I stayed a bit longer. How could I move? My family was in Ocala, and my father was getting sick, having had major strokes. I owned a house that I bought in 2010 that I thought was a great price at the time and was still upside down a bit as the market hadn't quite come back to where it was price point wise. And I owned a business in a community where I had grown roots for 14 years. I felt stuck. One thing is for certain I knew in my heart somehow I would make it out of Ocala before I retired or died!

Daniel's room was completely redone and became a den, and Stephen's room remained for him to come home to in Ocala to visit on occasion. I kept plugging along with real estate and helping to run my real estate company, with now about 8 Realtors attached. We never wanted to buy into a franchise because of all the guidelines and requirements of the franchisor and the cost. We wanted to be a small boutique brokerage that helped others and made it simple for Realtors, giving them the broker support needed training and to allow for them to keep more money in their own pockets. We offered a split less than most with no fees.

Chapter Four

With living and working in Ocala, every opportunity I had to vacation or have fun elsewhere was taken. I always dreamed of living the city life. I had made some trips to Tampa to visit my son and loved it. I've lived in many places over the years but never in a city where I could live in a high-rise and walk to work. Time kept marching on as the market slowly crept back upward.

My oldest son now moved to Colorado and was able to complete his schooling and become a Paramedic. 4 years later, my youngest son graduated from USF with his BA in Engineering-Civil. I was itching to move somewhere different and wanted to be close to at least one of my children. Daniel was already in Colorado and I had made many, many trips there and loved it!! It was definitely on my radar, and with it being a reciprocal state in real estate to Florida I was researching how to obtain a Broker's license there. All the while, still waiting to see what Stephen would do and where he would go after graduating.

The phone call came from my son Stephen, "I got good news, Mom! I was just offered an engineering position to start with a company located in Tampa, so I'm staying here."

That was the moment! I knew it was time to go, and without hesitation, I made the decision to move to downtown Tampa. I let my family know that I would only be an hour and a half away. I sold my house for $12,000 less than I bought it for and gave away my company to my partner. My father was not happy with my decision. I lost money on my house and gave away a company, knowing I had built this business from scratch and now have to go through the difficulty of starting over.

How hard can it be right? At this point, I did not know if I wanted to run and own a real estate company again and work general real estate at the same time. I was tired, tired of running and owning a company and working in real estate at the same time. I decided with the move that I would just hang my license with another brokerage as a broker's associate, which I had never done before, and just worry about myself and my own real estate. This is what I thought at the time.

I meandered downtown Tampa to find there were 2 small islands known as Harbour Island and Davis Island. I knew of Harbour Island and always loved it! I was lucky enough to find an apartment on Harbour Island. A beautiful 4th-floor loft apartment with a bedroom balcony view of the water and city looking across at the Amalie arena. To get to Harbour Island you have to come all the way through downtown Tampa and take one of two bridges onto the Island. It's really kind of swanky with a cute little downtown. It has its own little grocery store and a few restaurants right on the water. It felt like heaven on earth at the time. The river walk was amazing, too, and I walked everywhere. My favorite spot was

Jackson's, their little outdoor gelato and coffee shop. I loved the gelato, especially the chocolate flavor, and watching the beautiful sunset there was amazing.

I was still able to work my Ocala and Marion County Real Estate from Tampa. I could drive back and forth with no problem. That business in Marion County, my clients, family, friends, Realtors that I had built relationships with, and business partners were wonderful because they knew I had moved to Tampa and was working the Tampa Bay area, so the referrals would come, which was nice. The Ocala real estate and my experience kept my head above water while I tried to figure out Tampa Bay.

I found Davis Island by accident. I was just driving around to learn the area and came across a bridge, and as I went over the bridge, I came across a sign that said welcome to Davis Island. It has its own little downtown area with some restaurants along with cute shops and was much bigger than Harbour Island. I drove around the Island to see a little airport, a dog beach, a sailing club along with grocery stores, gas stations, and their cute little downtown, so I decided to pull into the downtown and take a stroll. The Island is beautiful, surrounded by water and you can see Harbour Island and the Port area.

As I was walking around peeking into shops I came across a Real Estate Brokerage. There was not one Real Estate Brokerage on

Harbour Island, and this was the only Brokerage on Davis Island. I'm looking at the listings posted in the window and peeking in when a lady comes in from across the street to ask if she can help me. I politely said no, thank you. I'm just browsing and looking around as I just moved here from Ocala. She asked me if I was looking to purchase a home, and I chuckled saying no, I just rented an apartment on Harbour Island. I let her know that I was actually looking around for a Brokerage to hang my broker license with. She immediately let me know that she with her husband were the owners and opened the door, saying, please come in and let's chat. I filled her in on my story, and she filled me in on theirs. It felt like a good fit at the time so I decided to hang my license there as a Broker Associate. They had their fees plus a sizeable split, but they did give me a desk to work from and the supplies needed. They offered no training and had a hand full of Realtors that would come and go and just did their own thing basically. They were super kind and helpful and introduced me to the sailing club as they were members and to some locals in the business that lived on Davis Islands as they did. Wonderful people to know.

I absolutely loved the office being a 2-minute drive from my Harbour Island apartment. My office in Ocala would take 20-30 minutes from my home.

As I started to venture out to work I realized I had to basically start over! The MLS in Ocala was for 1 County. I joined an MLS that encompassed 14 Counties. The Tampa Bay area to service was at a minimum of 3 Counties. Hillsborough, Pasco, and Pinellas. I came from a place where I had grown roots, known the county like the back of my hand, where my family was located and where most of my clients and relationships were to a place where I didn't know a soul, except for my son, having no knowledge of the areas or neighborhoods, etc. I had to go back to the basics of real estate to get going and get started again.

Chapter Five

I've always enjoyed being a part of my community and giving back in any way I can. One of the first things that I did to get myself more involved in the community and to meet people was to join the American Cancer Society's Cattle Baron Ball's committee as well as a group Known as HWOP, Hospice Women of Philanthropy. When I had my time in the military, I sat on the board of the officer's wife's club and also had been a part of the family support groups. When in Ocala, I sat on the board of the Marion County Literacy Council and was involved with donating and attending the Cattle Barron's Ball in Marion County. The Marion County Literacy Council is a non-profit organization to help adults to learn how to read so that it would create better opportunities for them. The reading level in Marion County at the time for adults was 5th grade. I just felt compelled to continue on in Tampa, somehow giving back.

I also joined the Tampa Club which was located on the 42nd floor of the Bank of America building. The Bank of America building is currently, along with the Regions Bank, the tallest building in downtown Tampa. The Tampa Club is known for being at the Top of Tampa. Beautiful views of the city, Islands, River, and water. I joined for personal and business. Big opportunity to meet other members and professionals in Tampa. Great opportunity for networking and making friends! I even managed to wiggle my way onto the membership committee. Another member and I coined the tagline, "Where members become friends and friends become family."

I always wanted to live in a city. I started to feel like I was finally living the life I had always dreamed about, living in a city and being able to walk to work. Tampa was a small city with everything a big city offers. With the Port of Tampa, Arts, Theatres, Shows, Hockey Team, Football Team, Airport, and a Live, Work, Play environment, I was definitely happy to be here and have no regrets about moving.

The first order of business when I arrived in Tampa was letting everyone know that I was a Real Estate Broker and serving the Tampa Bay Area and Ocala, Marion County including everything in between! If people do not know who you are, where you are, or what you do, along with the area you service, you'll see properties being listed by your friends with other Realtors. I sent out e-mail blasts, made phone calls, used social media to the hilt, and picked an area that I could farm for direct mail marketing. I even worked with a digital media company to create a magazine that was also getting direct mailed to my family, friends, clients, and business partners.

I would order a bunch of loose magazines that were

delivered to me so that I could hand them out along the way to people I would meet or leave at businesses. I would always support local small businesses and frequent certain places. The 2nd order of business was to start networking. Networking with professionals in my trade so that I could meet business partners to work with. I needed to know and meet Lenders, Home Inspectors, Photographers, Insurance agents, and the list goes on. Networking gets you out and about in your community and introduces you to potential business partners, clients, and friends. Sponsoring and holding events is another great opportunity to put yourself in front of people. I've always preached about Realtor Safety and Safety First. One of the first events I held was a Realtor Safety event at the Tampa Club.

Luckily, over the years, I had met some wonderful people who became my clients, and some clients even turned into friends that I still have today. I had a family that I had helped over the years whom I love because they were and still are awesome, and their brother was living and working in China. He contacted me and wanted to start Investing in some single-family residential homes that he could rent out in and around Tampa Bay to build a portfolio. I also had someone reach out to me from NY about purchasing an investment property in my area as he was looking into the future and was thinking of a move and would like to have something close to the water to move into a couple years down the road.

These clients were the ones that got me going in Tampa. Researching properties for them and learning about the market in Tampa, Clearwater, Saint Pete, etc. Doing real estate is what I love and how you learn! I'm certain that I took a phone call or two and lost some business due to me not being knowledgeable about the area I serviced so that was my mission—to get out and about and learn the areas. I started with Downtown Tampa and the islands since that's where I lived and worked. I walked the streets every day, looking around and learning. Then, I started crossing the bridges to learn about those areas. The first sale that I closed was for my NY investor, who purchased a condo in St. Pete. 45-minute drive from my office. My client from China purchased 3 properties, so I was on my way to making it.

I was still trying to find my way in Tampa, as I loved the owners of my brokerage, but I didn't like losing a big portion of my commissions and paying some fees. I just came from owning a Company where I kept 100% of what I made. I was offered a position as a Broker with another franchise office in Downtown Tampa keeping more of my money in my pocket and different opportunities to build a team and teach.

So, I jumped ship, giving that a try, and applied to the State of Florida for a Real Estate Instructors license. Honestly, this is the tougher of the real estate licenses to get with different requirements. In order to apply you need to have a Broker's license along with a minimum BA college degree along with 5 very recent sales that you were involved in to put in front of the State for evaluation. Luckily, I met all the requirements and was granted an instructor license to teach real estate. This was part of the opportunity I thought would happen with this new company and, honestly, it did not turn out the way I had hoped. At the same time, my long-time friend and Realtor moved to Tampa and hopped on board with me at this brokerage, and we started a team. Together we came up with a great team name to service Tampa Bay.

I decided after a year to move off of Harbour Island and secured a beautiful apartment on the 21st floor of a high rise in downtown Tampa. Now, I really felt like I was living the City life. I had an amazing view of the City, and the night lights were beautiful. I literally walked to work every day. Walked everywhere, it was wonderful. I saw so much change by walking the streets. New developments all over with high rises going up left and right. New areas that had nothing were coming alive. Tampanians were starting to know who I was and call out my name on the street. I loved it.

Again, I didn't like the current brokerage I was with and the opportunities that didn't happen, and I knew I could do better. My teammate wasn't happy either. The moment I was promised an opportunity with them, I worked diligently to make it happen, all while doing my own real estate. When the moment came to implement the agreement that we had made together, it was changed, and they thought I would sign anyway. I didn't. I went home that night and knew it was time once again for me to start my own boutique Brokerage. I had determined why I wanted to start my own brokerage again and that was to be better than the rest!

After a year and a half of floundering and a lot of learning, God placed in my heart that this was the time. It's what you are meant to do. A turning point in my life and career. I knew it would take time, effort, and a lot of work, but I felt good about it. Having your own brokerage means more money and more freedom but a heck of a lot more responsibility and liability. This time, I would do it all, fund it all on my own with no partners, and make sure my errors and omissions insurance was in place! After the nightmare with one partner and being in court for 3 years, I decided that if I couldn't do it on my own, I wouldn't. So, I did it on my own! My dad has now passed away but I knew he would be happy me owning my own company again with no partners.

So it began, the State approved my application and I was now the Owner and Broker of my own company once again. Starting over, but this time with a lot more knowledge of how to do it. Having some knowledge of my surrounding areas, knowing people and creating friendships. Setting it all up takes time. My goal was different this time; to build a company I could sell. I put in place my short-term goals and my 5-year business plan. Found an office suite on the 15th floor of the Park Tower building located downtown. I loved the walk to work life. To come and go as I pleased, to answer to no one but myself. Instead of working and building someone else's company I was now working to build my own.

I was working with other Realtors in Ocala, giving my business away on referrals. After a year and a half and now once again owning my own Brokerage/Company, I could basically do what I wanted with more autonomy needed to be successful, so I decided to rejoin the Ocala board and their MLS. The members there at OMCAR (Ocala Marion County Association of Realtors) were like, "Welcome Back!!" The first transaction under my new Company was for my mom in Ocala. After my dad passed away the 2 homes on 5 acres was too much to take care of for her. My sister, brother and I helped her scale down and I was able to find her a nice single family home on the same street as my brother, in the same neighborhood.

I once again had access to the MLS and could work that real estate myself and offer my clients more opportunities for exposure if they listed with me. The bigger the area you can service, the more successful you can be. Not having a partner or partners to answer to or to get permission from anyone to do anything was the golden ticket. It was me, myself, and I, and I was grateful to be at a point in my life to be able to do it. The hard work I put in prior to all of this is what enabled me to be in a better position. I still had a lot of hard work in front of me to reach my goals, to survive, and to be successful while enjoying life. I believe in a life-work balance, so as to not work your life away and get burnt out. Real Estate can consume you 24 hours a day, 7 days a week, nights and weekends if you let it. Technology over the years has changed the game in real estate. We are more accessible with social media. I learned that if I wanted to be successful I not only needed to be a real estate specialist but a marketing specialist more.

Once everything was in place, I used every social media platform I could and decided to advertise that I was looking to grow my company. There are two main reasons why Realtors will consider leaving the brokerages that they are at. The first reason is that they do not feel that they get the broker support that they were promised or need. Secondly, they consider leaving when they don't keep enough of their hard-earned commissions in their own pockets and pay too many fees to the brokerage and/or franchise.

I needed to be competitive with the commission, give the broker support needed, and offer the tools necessary for the Realtors to be successful. I wanted to teach, mentor, guide and help other Realtors to become successful because if they're a part of my company and they are successful, they contribute to my success. Now, the agent would be my client.

My 5-year business plan had four phases. Phase I - to start the company, grow and stabilize, adding 10-20 realtors with

Residential Real Estate. Phase II - Adding a Commercial Real Estate side and team for growth and stabilizing again. Phase III - To become a Real Estate School utilizing my Instructor License and, lastly, sell, all in 5 years. Having a business plan short term and long-term is always a good idea.

Put your thoughts, your goals, and your plans on paper. Where do you want to be and how do you want to grow at this moment in time? Even if you change things up along the way or, fall short along the way, or maybe you're ahead of schedule along the way, it doesn't matter because you can always, at the end of the five years, write a new five-year business plan.

My tagline is "helping others through my work." My motto is "Keep On Keeping On." With the right mindset, you can make anything happen. It's important to keep on keeping on, keep going because it means staying the course despite problems along the way or missteps. Keep on living out your best life to the best of your ability and it can take you to a place you never imagined in a short period of time. With integrity. With values and upholding the code of ethics.

Phase 1 of my business plan was completed and right on schedule, and phase 2 was completed and right on schedule. In between the 2 phases, COVID happened. I had about a year under my belt with my new company. It was totally up and running, with a handful of agents on board and completely funded with money spent on marketing, websites, and all the tools implemented. Finally, we had pending deals on the whiteboard to close, we were starting to gain that momentum. My realtors are nervous calling, asking me what they should do? Nervous about what was going to happen because the industry was changing due to COVID. My advice was to keep on keeping on letting those know that we were open for business and still working. We were helping through our work, and this was the time that people needed help. If other Realtors did not want to show homes, we would pay a nice referral fee to do so. We followed all of the CDC Guidelines and used the appropriate forms created by the State during this time. The real estate game was changing and definitely becoming more challenging.

I, too, was nervous. I had spent a year of my life building and funding this company. This was either going to make me or break me. Break me, it did not! We didn't know what would happen next. Thousands of people a month were moving to Florida and real estate in Florida went crazy. We had a housing shortage, builders couldn't keep up. Desperate buyers were buying homes sight unseen and paying way over list prices and appraised values. According to the U.S. Census Bureau, 243,933 people moved to Florida from July 1, 2020 to July 1, 2021, which was a net domestic migration. This was the fifth year in a row that Florida had the highest net migration in the country.

While everyone was not working or working from home, I went to my office every single day as we got very busy. Most of the office buildings in downtown Tampa closed down completely. Luckily mine did not. I loved walking to my office on the 15th floor every day and would be the only one there. Peaceful and Quiet.

Initially, COVID caused a lul in home sales but then, it quickly turned into a hot seller's market. Home values in Florida sky rocketed. Houses went under contract for over listing within minutes of them hitting the market under multiple offers. The timing of all this for my Company was good but it also came with its difficulties and challenges and we worked non-stop. I was constantly strategizing on how I could be different and more unique, more helpful so that we could better service our clients.

At this point, I am now a member of 7 boards and 3 MLS systems servicing a bunch of Florida Counties. I had a team of 20-plus realtors, residential and commercial, living in different areas so that we could service and specialize in those areas better. I was no longer doing general real estate myself but instead running the company as the sole owner and broker, giving my business to my Realtors to handle, which, of course, they did not have a problem with.

Time marched on, along with the hustle of real estate and my getting older. The company was doing well, sustaining. Realtors came on board, and some left. I was at the point of phase 3 of my business plan and checking into the idea of becoming a real estate school. At this time, I was introduced by a new friend to Islamorada in the Florida Keys.

At this point, I was looking for the slower pace of island life to gravitate towards, thinking of where I would want to retire. I made 3 trips to St. Croix, US Virgin Islands investigating. I loved it there, but every time I looked into becoming a Real Estate Broker there, I would hit road blocks. Even though St. Croix and the Virgin Islands are US territories with a Governor in place, they still have their own government and you cannot vote for the president. Shortly after my third trip to St. Croix, I made a trip to Islamorada in the Florida Keys. I met a wonderful man who lived in Islamorada while I was in Tampa and was told, "Come to Islamorada, and you may not wanna leave." Well, that statement was spot on!

I spent three nights at the Atlantic Bay resort in Tavernier, which is considered the upper keys and I was shown all around. I had a great time, and I couldn't wait to come back. 2 weeks later, I returned with a smile on my face. The joys of being in real estate, especially owning and being a broker without doing general real estate, we can work from anywhere! On the way down the second time the lightbulb went off inside of my head. The name of my prior company, Keys to the Bay Real Estate, fit perfectly. I could service the Florida Keys to Tampa Bay easily with no changes needing to be made. No plane rides, my son in Florida, and my family, so I would be in the same State. I'm already licensed in the state of Florida. All I have to do is open another branch office and join the board and MLS. Giving us all in the company more opportunity to service our clients better and for future business. My first trip to Islamorada was in August 2022. In November, three months later, I opened up a branch office in Islamorada.

The company now has three offices. The principal office was located in downtown Tampa. The commercial branch office was located in Lutz, and now another branch office in Islamorada. This would afford me the opportunity to work more in The Keys & South Florida and be in Islamorada more than I was. I would drive down every couple of weeks, and when in Islamorada, I did not want to leave. When I hit "the stretch," I hit my happy place. Joined the Islamorada Chamber of Commerce and, in April of 2023, had an official grand opening of the branch office and ribbon cutting. This office was my baby. Starting real estate here in a very tight-knit community was not easy. But, I was welcomed with open arms and on my way with a transaction in Marathon that closed, representing a seller with another Realtor and representing the buyer.

With that being said, I did not feel that I was doing my Realtors any justice being so far away most of the time. I prided myself on being a hands on broker. I still was, a lot more by phone and I still drove up to Tampa once a month to have our Company meetings and bring everyone together. I made the decision to follow my business plan and listed my Company for sale with a business broker friend located in Ocala. I did this to also better the Company that I built from the ground up and to make it better for the Realtors attached.

I interjected opening up the Islamorada office into my business plan, and it became phase 3, putting the real estate school and officially teaching on the back burner.

I loved Islamorada and the Florida Keys so much that I made a brave move to Islamorada in February 2023. The idea was to spend more time in Islamorada building this branch office and less time in Tampa. So now the travel was reversed, with me heading to Tampa every couple of weeks for a few days to take care of business there.

Phase 4, the sale of my brokerage, happened 2 months before its 5th anniversary and 2 months before the end of my 5-year business plan. Thankful. Grateful. Blessed.

My journey from a monotonous reality to a vibrant Paradise has been nothing short of extraordinary. Now, I'm fortunate enough to wake up every day in a place that most people only dream of visiting. My work is both fulfilling and purposeful, as I strive to make a positive impact on everyone I interact with. As I work toward my next goals in real estate, my dream has always been to be an inspiration to others, and I feel blessed to be living that dream.

I am very thankful for every little thing and for every person I have come across in my life! So many have inspired me❥

I have been a brand new agent, a part-time agent, an experienced full-time agent, a broker associate, a broker, a partner, a recruiter, and an owner in launching now four companies. I've mentored, guided, taught, and helped many others to be successful in real estate, to become new agents, experienced agents, team leaders, brokers and owners of their own brokerages! I've put in the long hours, nights, and weekends and had some sleepless nights. Not every deal gets to the closing table. I've made some mistakes along the way and learned some lessons the hard way.

That's why I'm writing this book! I was asked to speak a couple of years ago in front of a pitch group full of Realtors about telling my story of how I was there, and now I'm here and what it took to start and own my own brokerage. I've never even thought of speaking on that subject, never considered myself an expert by any means, and was a nervous wreck about speaking. How long do I have to speak was my first question? 30 minutes, I was told as the guest speaker. That's a long time, I thought to myself! However, I agreed and prepared a PowerPoint presentation.

As I was introduced to my peers, I decided to tell the audience that even though I had a presentation, I wasn't going to use it. I felt compelled to speak directly to them and not upward or backward to the screen behind me. I also felt that they would look at me and listen better rather than looking up at the screen. Eye contact was important. I didn't want to be boring or dry, so I interjected some humor in between and began to speak about my story and how I made it to the point of being asked to speak on this subject. I could have talked so much more. 30 minutes went by in a heartbeat! I was in awe when everyone stood up and clapped. Some were coming up to say my story inspired them. That's what it's all about. To help others and plant seeds. For those who want to better themselves and take real estate to another level. Thinking about starting a brokerage but not knowing how to or where to start. I was there. Thrown myself into the fire, sort of speak, learning and making mistakes. I want to help others who have taken the seed and planted it, and now want to water it to bloom!

My reason for starting a brokerage was not money-minded. Having a money mindset will get you nowhere. I truly wanted to help people. That was one of the reasons why I graduated with a BA in Psychology and a minor in Social Work. Who knew I would use that degree every day in real estate. In my recruiting, I would ask questions. I would not just sign on any Realtor to my company. Every Realtor I accepted and attached to my company would be a direct reflection of me. Having a non-money mindset and integrity, ethics, morals, and values while wanting to help others is what I was searching for.

One bad apple can ruin the bunch and put your broker license on the line along with the brokerage. And I can say that has happened to me. I hired someone to help recruit and grow the company as a team leader, and instead, he ended up disrupting causing grief, and had to be let go. I did lose a few Realtors at the time. You can start a real estate brokerage without a broker's license, but legally, one person has to have a Broker license and be the broker of record. In my company, that was me. Deciding on what type of brokerage you want to be and what size is important. Establishing what your dream brokerage looks like is a good first step. Owning a boutique or franchise brokerage is yet another decision, writing down the costs, pros, and cons of each. I decided to not buy into a franchise and wanted to be a small boutique brokerage with a family feel. Everyone on board was always willing to help the others when needed-

The next level takes some courage. The next step in your journey demands boldness and determination. This is when you have that courage to take a risk and push past your comfort zone.

Chapter Six

This is where I want to help those wanting to take their Real Estate career to the next level. Also to inspire all entrepreneurs to do the same. I'm offering some steps and advice here on how I got from being there to being here… from being a part-time Realtor to becoming a Broker - Owner starting and launching a real estate brokerage to selling it in less than 5 years. Do you want to do as I being a Broker and Owner or maybe just an Owner of your own Real Estate Brokerage? One of the most fundamental decisions will be to the company's ownership. In order to start, you need to ask yourself some questions and have the answers ready before giving yourself the green light. This can all happen rather quickly, too.

Make certain that you qualify to launch a Brokerage before even getting started. Do you have a Broker's license? Do you need a Broker's license? Advancing your Real Estate career to new heights requires unwavering dedication, persistence, and resilience. It's not for those who are easily deterred by obstacles along the way. If you feel you want to take your business and career to the next level, then follow these twelve steps - my helpful guide to help you get there if it is truly something you desire to do.

Step One: Determine Your Why

We need to clarify and understand our why in order to grow. Your why is the most important step and the reason it is first on the list. Your why is your motivation to do what it is you want to do. What is your motivation? Our why includes your own motivation for doing what you do or for what you want to do. What are your values and passions? Why do you want to take it to the next level? Why do you want to launch a Brokerage? Why do you want to be an owner of your own real estate brokerage? What value will you provide? Once you know your why, you will be able to envision exactly what you want to accomplish. There are risks involved, of course, and it will take time, effort, knowledge, and money to take it up a notch. Do you want to be the Owner and Broker? Do you want to be an Owner and hire a Broker? Do you want a partner or multiple partners? Why? Write it down. Write down why it is important to you at this point in your life to want to take your career to the next level or to maybe start a Real Estate Brokerage. Knowing your why is the secret sauce. It can help you find your purpose and inspire others. Not only does this motivate you but it also helps you stay focused and to stay on track. Success of any kind or at any level takes time, dedication and hard work. Your why is that force that keeps you going and will keep you motivated. Before you can move on you really must clarify your why or you will just be wasting your time and energy. So, write it down! Once it is written you can then look at it constantly for inspiration.

Step Two: Make The Decision

You have written down your why, so now it's time to consider the situation. Explore all your options and weigh the pros and cons. Ask questions if you need to and ask for support. When you decide to make a change and take your Real Estate game to the next level, you open yourself up to a world of new possibilities. You will be able to discover new strengths and abilities within yourself and reach places you never thought were accessible. This journey will lead you to new paths of success, which will, in turn, lead to a new chapter in your life book. By doing so, you will be able to reach new heights and achieve things you never thought were possible.

Are you ready to get started? If you know your why and decide YES! This is what I want to do. Then, write down your goals, your vision, and your mission. Your mission, too, is your why. Your purpose for existing. Why are you starting a brokerage? What is the purpose of the company? What will it look like? Where should the company be in the future? Will you lead or hire someone to lead? Leadership is important. Leadership can help you achieve success as well as those on your team. I chose to lead and to lead by example. I created a shared vision that gave us all a sense of purpose and a sense of direction. Your title doesn't make you a leader. Your integrity, actions, attitude, empathy, drive, and behavior will earn the respect of those on your team or those wanting to be on your team.

If you have made the decision to do this, to take your career to the next level then you need to stay committed. Being committed will give you what you need to turn this dream into a reality and sets a good example for those that will join you. Staying committed will get you to where you want to be. Making the decision is basically making the first move-you've decided to take the chance!

Come up with your inspiring tagline. Mine is "Helping Others Through My Work." Write down the standards and your values that you want to follow. Put it all on paper. Your goals need to be solid and somewhat attainable, don't get crazy with putting too much on yourself at the beginning. That's why writing short-term and long-term goals is important. You'll be surprised at how easily you will manifest and meet your goals. And, if they are not all met that's ok. Draw up a 5-year business plan that outlines your goals for the next 5 years. It's basically a roadmap to help you navigate your way to reaching those goals.

Step Three: Money

Do you have the money needed to start? To get a brokerage started there is going to be a cost. Are you a working Realtor with an income stream? Have you banked money? I had banked enough money to get me going for at least the first year. If I did not make one cent, I knew I could live and pay my bills. Success is never guaranteed, and the first 2 years of a new business are the most difficult. Real Estate can be squirrely - the market can shift as it is known to do. The economy could take a dump. You can be sued, and the list goes on.

My suggestion is to have a minimum of 1 year of business and personal expenses in the bank, which will make this process a lot easier with less stress. I funded my company myself. If you cannot, there are, of course, other options available to you to get started. You may want to pull in a partner that you trust that has money to fund. There are loans out there as well to finance new business ventures that you may qualify for. Leveraging money is always a good idea. Leverage is when you use borrowed funds. It is an investment strategy that can also build your business credit. Depending on what your brokerage will look like and size, you will need $10,000 at a minimum to get started, possibly more. The first company I started took $10,000 to get going. The third company more, about $30,000.

Step Four: Franchise or Boutique

What kind of brokerage do you want to be? One maybe that is Nationally recognized and has their branding in place? There is a cost to that and guidelines that you have to follow. There is less flexibility in decision-making. There are pros and cons to each. The National Association of Realtors (NAR) reported Less REALTORS® had an affiliation with a franchised company (39%) than with an independent company (55%). 6% was reported as other.

I decided on the independent boutique so that I could be creative and have my own branding. I also didn't have to worry about territories. I did not want to have to live by anyone else's rules or answer to a franchisor and pay them for that. I wanted to give more personalized service to the Realtors on my team. A boutique brokerage gave me the autonomy to be creative in my brand design and messaging. I proudly built a brand that I was able to sell on my own in less than 5 years. Despite the trend of large businesses, most of our nation's businesses are still small. I proved that there is still a place in the market for small, independent real estate companies. In my experience, Realtors like to work for boutique brokerages because they receive dedicated attention and don't feel like they are just a number.

Step Five: Determine Where

Research. Where do you want to service, and where do you want to have an office? This office will be considered your principal and primary office. Registered with the DBPR. Do you want to be a virtual brokerage or have a brick-and-mortar brokerage? I always wanted an office to go to, to work from, to offer Realtors. The costs will be higher going this route, and finding space where you want to be is important. My advice, start small. I started simply with an office suite in downtown Tampa that had everything I needed and met all the state requirements for $500.00 a month. My name was on the door, and I had closings in the conference rooms. You can go as simple as you need to start or go as big as you feel to grow into. You want your office and the area you service to be where you are incredibly knowledgeable not only about the area but also about the market. Start small, and then, if you wish, down the line, you can branch out. I started with 1 office and added 2 branch offices.

Going virtual is also an option. Overhead would be lower, for sure. But, you would not have any walk-in business or signage in your market area, which means no brand awareness on the street. You would have to rely on advertising and social media for brand awareness. I always enjoyed working from an office location every day. It's an opportunity to meet more people and gain more business. I laugh because I would meet so many people in the elevator!! I always introduced myself and asked what they did for work. I have a preferred lender that is awesome, and when asked how we met, we say we met in an elevator!

Step Six: Implement Tools and Branding

Branding is so important because in my opinion it is a direct reflection of who you are and the image you want to portray. Today, branding is more complex than ever, it is not just a name and a logo. Your brand will help you connect on an emotional level. My advice is to create a brand unique to you and the values you want to represent. Your brand should differentiate you from others. Your brand should be recognized and remembered! Strong branding creates the reputation and establishes trust and credibility. Make certain your branding is consistent across all marketing platforms too. Basically, your personal branding will build a connection with your audience that is meaningful and memorable creating value which will set you apart.

Implement all the tools and systems needed to make your job easy and your company successful. Also, implement the tools and systems needed to help the agents you recruit and have on board to be successful. At a minimum, you will need a Website, CRM, and Lead Generation along with transaction management and accounting capabilities.

Step Seven: Communicate Your Vision

Creating your brand is communicating your vision. Create your brand. The company/brokerage name is the most important. My advice is to always make certain the name you chose for your company has an available domain. Go online to check, and if it is available, claim it and buy it. I owned Keys to the Bay Real Estate. I owned the domain keystothebay.com. I am now Madeline Rousseau Real Estate and own MadelineRousseau.com. Find a graphic artist to work with who can express what you want and are looking for. You are your brand. Make it personal and professional. Create your logo. The 2nd most important item in branding. This is the visual representation of everything you and your brokerage stand for. Research your competitors differentiating yourself. Create your tagline or slogan.

"Helping others through my work" "We hold the key to all of your real estate needs." Show the world why you will succeed. Once completed, prepare your marketing plan. Identify key target markets for the area of your primary office and for the area you want to service. Your agents, recruit, and teammates should also portray your message and your business model using your branding. It's ok for them to be unique and have their own branding as they are considered 1099 employees and business owners of their own company but make sure they integrate you and your branding as well. There are actually legal guidelines set by the State that have to be followed when realtors brand themselves along with their brokerage. Some Brokerages do not allow realtors to brand themselves. I did because if you don't they eventually will and will go out on their own. Allowing them to brand themselves helps with agent retention. Become a social media expert or hire someone to do it for you. You have to have a presence today on line. Facebook, LinkedIn, Instagram, Google, etc., learn how to run and optimize these platforms, and they will provide you with leads and business and keep you in front of thousands of people, clients, etc.

Step Eight: Execute A Brokerage Business Plan

This is the foundation of your business. You've already created a business plan for yourself. Now, create one specific to the brokerage. This business plan will help you run your business. Short term 1 year and a 5 year. It will guide you through each stage of managing your business, and you should use it as a road map. Here is where you show and state your path to success. Write a summary and describe your company and how it will operate. In this plan, you can show a financial projection. Show how you will recruit realtors and a number goal. How will you pay them, splits and fees? This is important to have in place. The services you will implement and offer. Realtors, as independent 1099 contractors, the brokerage they choose to hang their license with will have a huge impact on their own business as well as your business. Encourage them as well to write it all down and create their own business plans.

Step Nine: Lead Generation

Now that everything is in place and hopefully up and running you will need to work on lead generating. Offering leads keeps your realtors on board happy. There are platforms that you can get into with no cost for the leads and paying a referral fee when closed. These are pay-at-closing leads and the way those like to start when monies are limited. Or, you can pay for leads upfront. Make certain your website chosen integrates with your lead gen. You'll have a back end to manage so that you can see every that is going in with those leads and the realtors working them.

Step Ten: Recruiting

Once your lead generation is in place and all of the hard work that we spoke about prior to this point is in place, it's time to grow if that is what you so desire. Recruiting and getting them to stay is a full time job and constant. You can do this yourself, or you can hire someone to do it for you. Recruitment is the process of seeking out and hiring Realtors to join you and your company. When you bring a Realtor on and attach them and their license to your real estate brokerage, then you will need to onboard them.

So, you will want to make certain all of the paperwork needed is ready for them to sign. I always had an employee file. I always had a simple salesperson agreement and a W9 ready for signature. Grabbed a copy of their real estate license and driver's license for my files as well. I would ask for a professional photo and a bio so that I could promote them. A first set of business cards and a name badge were ordered by me for them. You will need an onboarding system in place. Once they are on boarded, then you can add them to your systems like your company websites, lead gen and transaction management. You must familiarize yourself with recruitment fundamentals. It's an important part of growing your business. It will help you hire and find talented and experienced Realtors. It will help you hire those with the same values and principles. It might be smart to look at recruitment strategies from other Real Estate Brokerage because they are your competitors, and you want to be able to offer a competitive compensation plan.

Being involved in your own recruitment is great because you get to meet new people and those in your profession. The National Association of Realtors states, "The need for greater diversity in the real estate industry is apparent. Brokers can cultivate a more diverse and inclusive workplace by taking an intentional approach to their recruiting strategies. Connect with diverse candidates through targeted job fairs and mentoring opportunities. As a leader, understand that the commitment to diversity and inclusion comes from the top."

A great way to recruit is to host Realtor Events, host trainings and classes. Attend industry events yourself. Promote your culture, network. Use social media. Be competitive and offer to help agents build their own brand. As a Broker and an Owner my recruiting tagline was "The agent is my client."

Step Eleven: Management

I managed my brokerage myself completely. I managed the office and the Realtors. It can be difficult and overwhelming. Management is mostly about managing your people. There is a human element in everything. The more you grow, the more time will be needed. If you feel you don't have the time to completely manage yourself as I did, and If you have the resources, hiring a manager can help.

My advice is to lead from the heart and don't be a micro-manager. Set the example. Have integrity, be honest, and give respect. Give the agents on board the training they need and also autonomy along with some trust. Encourage your Realtors to complete their post-licensing continuing education credits before the deadlines have passed. And, keep an eye on their license expiration dates to remind them to renew their real estate licenses through the State. It is helpful to make certain your Realtors take the MLS classes with your local board that you are a member of or if a member of many boards, whichever board - MLS the Realtor belongs to.

Agents can't enter listings quickly or accurately if they don't know how, and they need this information from the add/edit MLS classes. The MLS that I belonged to made this course mandatory, or the agent could not add or edit listings in the MLS. Taking an MLS class will also help agents do research for their comparative market analyses and their property searches for their buyers. Knowledge is power. Most have orientation and basic MLS classes. Encourage your agents to attend closings.

This is important, and a lot is learned at the closing table. You will have to stay on top of everything at all times, that will keep you out of trouble and out of the court system. Supervision is getting tougher as we move away from the traditional office environment into more of a virtual work from anywhere environment. I'll admit there were times when I literally winged it to success! But I would not recommend that! Make sure all your legal bases are covered, and that you have a great attorney you can call when needed. The Realtors on board and future Realtors want to see that you have structure and a clear direction.

It's a very vulnerable place to be in and will require your time, courage, and some personal sacrifice. No matter what time it was or what day when one of my Realtors called I answered my phone. I always tried to be unique and look for new ways to do things. Thinking outside of the box. I aspired to inspire them. As a leader and manager of your own real estate brokerage, you have a powerful influence over your group of Realtors, and they are looking up to you. You will have many duties, but the most important will be to motivate your people. Guiding them, mentoring them, and helping them to be successful is very rewarding. When they are successful, you and your brokerage will be successful.

When the company becomes open for business, it takes on a life of its own with the wheels in motion. It becomes propelled by people, processes and systems put in place. Many things happen all at one time. Taking your Real Estate career to the next level is not for the weak. It's a journey meant only for those who possess the inner strength and resilience to persevere through any challenges that come their way. Not every Realtor or Broker wants to do it, but if you do, it will change your life, and you will never be bored!

Step Twelve: Networking

This is so important! It is a vital part of building a successful and thriving business. It's not only about business networking but it's about making friends and building relationships in business. A lot of times, the relationships cross over to personal, too. You will establish meaningful connections with people who will, in turn, want to help you succeed and reach your goals. I started 2 networking groups myself. I started a BNI chapter from scratch in Tampa called BNI Top of Tampa, which is still up and running today!! I gave that 2 years of my life and put in a lot of time and effort to build it and for it to be successful! I was the original founder and first president once it launched. I believe I held the record for the fastest launch—and held the Residential Real Estate seat.

One profession per seat, and it had strict guidelines due to the BNI franchise. BNI is huge and global. My chapter was wonderful, but I gave it up after 2 years as it was another full-time job. My tagline for my networking groups was always "where members become friends and friends become family." After BNI, I started a networking company and a networking group called Bright Ideas Group. When I sold Keys to The Bay Real Estate, I included this networking group that I founded with the help of 2 others and led by hosting 2 events per month to bring us together.

We had exclusive member only events, happy hours and lunches. We also had open events, happy hours and lunches where members could invite guest that we thought could benefit from the group or maybe join the group. Twice a month, we met, socialized and gave a 30-second infomercial on who we were, what we did and what a good referral would be. We all took care of and looked out for one another and used each other for our own personal needs as referring to family and friends. We got to know one another more by having one to one meetings outside of our regular scheduled events. This was a more intimate setting where we could really get to know one another and how we can best help and help each other grow our companies.

When someone from my networking group called me, I immediately answered my phone!! These people, business professionals and strategic partners were the ones I knew, liked and trusted. You can access new opportunities, exchange ideas, get advice, increase visibility, and boost your confidence and public speaking through networking. As you build these relationships, you establish a sense of value and worth. It may even help create more avenues for your business. Having a good network is really important, especially in real estate. You become a valuable source to your clients, and they will come to you when they need other services, like a plumber when they have a leaky sink, which helps your clients continually think of you and keeps you in front of them, too.

I sold my brokerage within 5 years. Building a business to sell and actually selling it is amazing. Seeing your vision come into play and seeing your business plan fall into place. My business was profitable from day one. I loved running and owning it. Selling my brokerage wasn't about cashing out. I followed my heart and the timing of my life. I took my career to the next level, and now it's about growth and shifting. Evolving as an entrepreneur and as a person.

There are no magic answers, and guarantees are few, but the one certain thing is change. I see change as an opportunity. I'm ready for the next and the thrill of a new project and to maybe start something new, like writing and publishing this book! I've noticed my energy shifting now that I'm not running a company day to day. Reflecting on my journey and wanting to share my story. I know other opportunities are waiting for me in my real estate career. I'm eager to speak to those in a position to maybe take their career to that next level. To show how I was there and now I'm here. To share how I Built and Sold a Real Estate Brokerage and how I can help you do the same.

From a young age, I have always known that I wanted to

make a difference in the world. Now that I am living my dream in paradise, I am able to do just that. Through my work, I am able to help others and inspire them to chase their own dreams. I believe that we all have the power to create positive change, and I am committed to using my skills and resources to do just that.

Making a change and upping your real estate game is a powerful decision that can have a profound impact on your life. By taking this step, you will be able to discover new strengths and reach places you never thought were possible, leading you to new paths of success and a new chapter in your life book. Success is created from within. Success is not derived from money. It is derived from following your heart, having courage and trusting in yourself and your abilities. You have to believe that you are capable of going the distance and landing up where you want to be. I landed up living in paradise which is where I wanted to be! A new chapter will hopefully be filled with growth, achievement, and personal development, allowing you to reach your full potential. Success stems from a "Happy Outcome."

Madeline Rousseau-Broker/Owner/Instructor

Madeline Rousseau Real Estate

Islamorada, FL 33036

352-274-2407 Cell

www.MadelineRousseau.com

Chapter Seven:
Focus on the Future

Neglecting to monitor the future of business will lead to significant setbacks. We operate in a constantly evolving society where social media trends fluctuate, consumer preferences shift, and what proves effective today may not yield similar results tomorrow.

Be calm and ready to take on the future.

If you choose to elevate your career, dive right in with unbridled optimism and enthusiasm!

It is crucial to have a clear vision for the future and not just focus on the present moment. "As Fundera's statistics show, a staggering number of small businesses fail within their first decade, with 20% failing in the first year, 30% in the second year, and 50% after five years." To avoid this, you must, as a business owner, invest in future thinking and planning.

Think about the future of marketing. Before email and social media, businesses relied on paper mailers, cold calls, and door-to-door sales.

Newspaper ads and leaflet drops may seem outdated, but they were effective 10-20 years ago. To succeed in today's crowded online market, businesses need a future-proof marketing strategy that includes Google AdWords, email marketing, and staying up-to-date with social media trends. Today, as Real Estate Brokers and Owners, we need to be marketing specialists as well as Real Estate specialists and embrace AI. Think about outside technology and how your business and company can shift when huge changes come into play. Technology moves fast. We can almost not keep up with it! Keeping up with the changes in technology, economy, culture, and globalization is no easy feat.

I always say you have to be a chameleon and be able to change and adapt. The one constant in real estate, as in life, is change. The capacity to adapt and evolve like a chameleon can be a valuable asset for personal and business development and growth. By observing their surroundings, learning from trial and error, and changing color to blend in or express their mood, chameleons embody versatility. Similarly, we can cultivate these skills through observation, experimentation, and introspection, leading to greater adaptability and resilience in diverse situations. Businesses have the capability to envision and materialize products and experiences that cater to the needs of their clients. If you want to thrive, adapting swiftly to new laws and regulations, shifting market conditions and developing chameleon-like adaptability is your key to success in a fast-changing world.

From year one my company was profitable because of my forward thinking. I anticipated, and I prepared. I spent a considerable amount of my time and energy understanding past cycles and current market trends. The sale of my Real Estate Brokerage has given me yet another opportunity to rise and thrive in an ever-changing industry. I've also given that company a new way to thrive by adding more value to what the new owners wanted to add. I wouldn't have just sold my baby to just anyone. Giving me another opportunity for self-elevation with my new company, Madeline Rousseau Real Estate.

As you elevate, remember to be social, I was always the face of the company that I owned. Get out there and meet people, pick up the phone and call people. Treat people in business the way you would want to be treated. Set the example for the future generation of Realtors, Brokers and Company owners, as well as always giving back by getting involved in your community. And always have integrity! Real Estate often deals with investors, buyers, sellers and large sums of money along with emotional ties. A successful Realtor/Broker/Owner who has integrity will not lie, cheat, steal or mislead. We should always ensure all parties are treated fairly and that everything in a transaction is transparent. Having integrity is just as important in life as well!!

Acting honestly and with integrity and doing the right thing will always build character and will earn you respect. If anyone were to inquire about me I don't believe there is one person that could ever put me in a negative light, ever! Even when those who tried to my reputation was and is so stellar that it only hurt those trying to.

My people all across the board who know me would know better!

We all know that the struggle is real! 3 words come to mind about myself and my success. Resilience, Persistence and Determination. Persistence is key, never giving up and staying committed. Being able to handle stress is a must. Real Estate is probably up there on the list when it comes to the most stressful careers. I always told my mom over the years that I might have picked the wrong profession for my anxiety! High-stakes negotiating, bidding wars, bad inspections, low appraisals, sink holes and the list goes on. If you want to be at the top of your game and career, learning how to deal with stress is a must. Being calm always is key and knowing how to solve problems! I always say we are Realtors, aka problem solvers!

It is important to continually focus on the future and maintain a future, focused mindset continuously striving towards future goals.

Building and achieving success can seem like a daunting task at times. I have proven that it is possible as I shared my story here and how I built my success basically from the ground up. I started later in life and as a novice. I became a respected Broker/Owner and a respected leader. Have faith in yourself and your experience and abilities!! Have the confidence to elevate! I hope you make your mark in the world!

About The Author

Madeline Rousseau

Broker/Owner/Instructor

A highly qualified real estate professional and Broker with many years of experience. Although born in New York, she was raised in Ft. Lauderdale and calls Florida home. She then moved to Marion County in 1985 and obtained a BA in Psychology with a minor in Social Welfare from UCF. Even to this day her education and degree serves her well in real estate. Having obtained her real estate license in 2009, when the market turned difficult and buyers and homeowners needed help most, she learned the industry the hard way and specialized in residential short sales.

Currently, she not only handles residential real estate, but also home rentals, new home construction, vacant land and commercial real estate. Madeline LOVES helping those wanting to sell their homes as well as matching buyers to their dream homes. The process and relationships are very rewarding with often times clients becoming friends. In 2014, Madeline decided to obtain a broker's license and recently made a major life change moving to Islamorada in the Upper Florida Keys in order to pursue her dream of having her own company in Florida servicing South Florida and The Florida Keys.

Madeline proves that she is dedicated to her clients, but also aggressive and will get the job done by diligently guiding her clients through the buying and selling process. A firm believer in Integrity, Honesty and Listening, Madeline provides expert knowledge, dedication and is committed to find perfect properties for her buyers. Madeline has been a single mom to two wonderful boys who are now grown men. They are the light of her life along with her grandson! She has a great family, a lot of wonderful friends, business partners and clients with whom she stays close to for they have supported her and made her the successful real estate agent/broker/owner she is today!